INTRODUCING THE STAR OF THIS BOOK

★ LEAELLYNASAURA ★

(lee-EL-in-UH-sawr-ah)

DID YOU KNOW...

that *Leaellynasaura*, a turkey-sized herbivore, survived in a part of Australia that was much further south in the early Cretaceous period. Back then, it was attached to a vast polar continent. Chilly!

Leaellynasaura means 'Leaellyn's lizard'

SETTING THE SCENE

It all started around 231 million years ago (mya), when the first dinosaurs appeared, part-way through the Triassic Period.

The Age of the Dinosaurs had begun, a time when dinosaurs ruled the world!

Scientists call this time the

MESOZOIC ERA
(mez-oh-zoh-ic)

and this era was so long that they divided it into three periods.

TRIASSIC
←····· lasted 51 million years ·····→

JURASSIC
←····· lasted 56 million years ·····→

252 million years ago

201 million years ago

Leaellynasaura lived during the Cretaceous Period from 118 – 110 million years ago.

CRETACEOUS

←·················· lasted 79 million years ··················→

145 million years ago   66 million years ago

WEATHER REPORT

The world didn't always look like it does today. Before the dinosaurs, and during the early part of the Mesozoic Era, the land was all stuck together in one supercontinent called Pangaea. Over time, things changed and by the end of the Cretaceous Period the land looked like this.

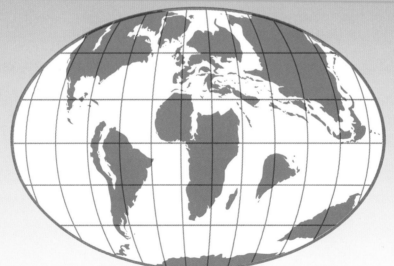

CRETACEOUS 66 mya

Name comes from the Latin word for 'chalk'

TRIASSIC

Very hot, dry and dusty

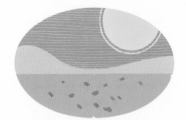

JURASSIC

Hot, humid and tropical

CRETACEOUS

Warm, wet and seasonal

During the Cretaceous Period part of Australia was near the South Pole and during the cold, dark winters the ground was permanently frozen.

HOMETOWN

Here's what's been discovered so far and where...

AUSTRALIA
DINOSAUR COVE

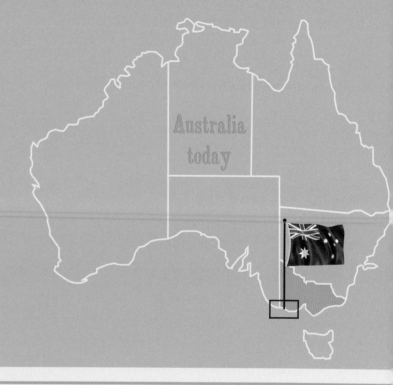

Australia today

Australia 110 mya

Antarctic Circle

Antarctica 110 mya

PALAEONTOLOGISTS
**THOMAS RICH &
PATRICIA VICKERS-RICH**
NAMED LEAELLYNASAURA
IN 1989

Fragmentary skeletons,
teeth and skull bones

Whilst mining for fossils in a narrow strip of rock in Dinosaur Cove, Victoria, in the southern tip of Australia, Thomas Rich and Patricia Vickers-Rich, with a group of miners and volunteers, discovered the partial remains of a dinosaur that they named after their daughter, Leaellyn.

From the age of 10 months, Leaellyn accompanied her parents on fossil digs and even participated in the discovery of the bones of *Leaellynasaura* a few years later.

VITAL STATISTICS

During the Cretaceous Period, in the polar region of Australia, plant life was hard to come by during the wintry months, yet *Leaellynasaura* survived and thrived in this harsh climate.

Let's look at *Leaellynasaura* and see what's special, quirky and downright amazing about this dinosaur!

LEAELLYNASAURA

40 cm tall from toe to hip

At 40 cm tall and as one of the smaller dinosaurs from the Cretaceous Period, *Leaellynasaura* would easily fit through a door. However, *Leaellynasaura* is only known from juvenile remains and so as an adult would have been bigger, but still able to fit through a door easily!

DOOR
2 m high

hip height
measurement

BUS Traditional double decker

Length: up to 1.2 m

Height: 40 cm from toe to hip

Weight: 5 - 10 kg

LEAELLYNASAURA

Length: **11 m** Height: **4.5 m** Weight: **8 tonnes** (empty)

TRAINING BIKE

Length: **40 cm** Height: **50 cm** Weight: **4 kg**

MOUSE

SCARY
SCALE

How does
Leaellynasaura
rate?

NOT SCARY

 1 **2**   **3**   **4** **5**

Compared to many other dinosaurs,
Leaellynasaura was small, light and
agile, so able to run fast through
the forest to evade the big polar
carnivores!

EEEEEKKKK!!!

Read on to find who
might have scared
Leaellynasaura!

6 7 8 9 10

SCARY

BRAININESS

When dinosaurs were first discovered
they were thought to be quite stupid!

Then a few scientists thought that some dinosaurs had
a second brain close to their butt! That's now just a myth.

Today scientists know that dinosaurs had one brain and were
intelligent for reptiles. Some were among the most intelligent
creatures alive during the Mesozoic Era, although
still not as smart as most modern mammals.

By looking at the:

Body size

Size
of the
brain

Sense
of
smell

Eyesight

scientists can tell how they rated against each other...

WHERE DOES LEAELLYNASAURA, A PLANT-EATING DINOSAUR, STAND ON THE 'BRAINY SCALE'?

TROODON
(TRU-oh-don)

10/10
CARNIVORE
(brainiest)

T. REX
(tie-RAN-oh-SAW-russ rex)

9/10
CARNIVORE

tiny!

LEAELLYNASAURA
↗ (lee-EL-in-UH-sawr-ah)

7/10
HERBIVORE

IGUANODON
(ig-WAHN-oh-DON)

6/10
HERBIVORE

STEGOSAURUS
(STEG-oh-SAW-russ)

4/10
HERBIVORE

DIPLODOCUS
(di-PLOD-oh-KUSS)

These dinosaurs are drawn to
scale in relation to each other!

2/10
HERBIVORE
(not so brainy)

SPEED-O-METER

SLOW

1 2 3 4 5

Small, bipedal (ran on two
back legs) and agile, the
perfect combination for being
able to nip through the dense
forests of polar Australia.

6 7 8 9 10

FAST

There are lines in bones (like rings in trees) called LAGs – Lines of Arrested Growth. These can tell scientists if a creature hibernates (sleeps through the winter) or not. The LAGs in *Leaellynasaura* show that its growth slowed during colder times, probably because there was little or no sunshine, and so less food around. Because of this, palaeontologists think *Leaellynasaura* didn't hibernate, but stayed active all year round, despite the polar conditions.

This has opened up the debate about whether dinosaurs were warm-blooded, cold-blooded, or even a combination of both. *Leaellynasaura* might have been warm-blooded, so it could have regulated its own body temperature through the chilly winter.

Dinosaur burrows, made at the same time *Leaellynasaura* was alive, have been found in rocks near where this dinosaur was discovered. Some of these burrows could have been made by *Leaellynasaura* to escape from the extreme cold.

The tail was three times the length of *Leaellynasaura*'s body and was made up of over 70 vertebrae (back and tail bones), making it super-long and flexible.

It could have been used to steer, while speeding through the forest, or for display, to attract a mate. This super-long tail may also have curled around its body to help keep it warm.

Extra large optic lobes (the part of the brain that works with the eyes) show that this dinosaur's brain was great at seeing in the near-darkness. This would help it look for food during the night and the day.

TEETH

Despite the lack of deadly teeth and claws, *Leaellynasaura* was able to survive and even thrive in a harsh climate.

The small, high-crested, leaf-shaped cheek teeth would have been shed as they wore down, to be replaced by new teeth, as was the case for all dinosaurs.

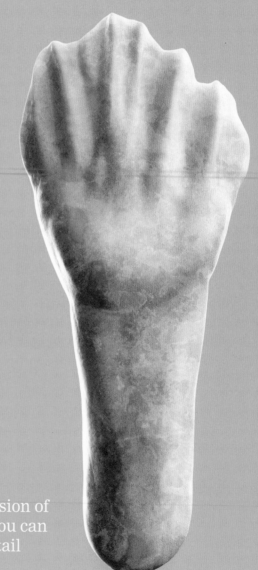

5 mm

Tooth to scale

Over-sized version of the tooth so you can see the detail

DIET

Leaellynasaura would have used its beak-like mouth to nip at low-lying ferns and horsetails.

During the winter months it would have hunted on the forest floor for any plants or berries that weren't frozen.

WHO LIVED IN THE SAME NEIGHBOURHOOD?

Here are two dinosaurs that lived in the same part of what is now Australia as *Leaellynasaura*…

THEROPOD
(THER-oh-pod)

A few isolated bones, including some from large theropods, have been found around the same areas as *Leaellynasaura* and are of the same age. One is known from fragments, was also discovered by Thomas Rich and Patricia Vickers-Rich and is called *Timimus* (tih-MY-muss) after their son, Tim, and a famous climatologist, Dr Tim Flannery!

MUTTABURRASAURUS
(mutt-ah-BURH-ah-SAW-russ)

Although the bones of *Muttaburrasaurus* have never been discovered in the same area as *Leaellynasaura*, it lived at roughly the same time. They may have met as they both lived in forested areas, although there was little to fear from this 8 m long dinosaur – it only ate plants.

WHICH ANIMAL ALIVE TODAY IS MOST LIKE LEAELLYNASAURA?

Like *Leaellynasaura*, squirrels have very impressive tails. A squirrel's tail is about the same length as its body and can be wrapped around its body to keep it warm in the winter.

Both use their tails for balance and steering – *Leaellynasaura* to steer as it ran, a squirrel to help it balance as it leaps across treetops or does a high-wire act on a telephone wire!

Interestingly, neither hibernate, but squirrels burrow to keep themselves out of the chilly wintry weather and it's possible that *Leaellynasaura* did too.

WHAT'S SO SPECIAL ABOUT LEAELLYNASAURA?

WHEN LEAELLYNASAURA LIVED

CRETACEOUS 118 – 110 MYA

TOOTH SIZE

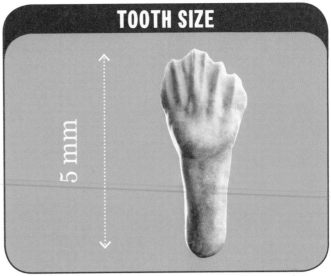

5 mm

WEIGHT

10 KG

FAST OR SLOW?

SPEED

out of 10

6

THE BEST BITS!

DISCOVERED, SO FAR

FRAGMENTARY SKELETONS, TEETH AND SKULL BONES

HOW FRIGHTENING?

SCARY

1

MEAT OR PLANTS?

SPECIAL BITS

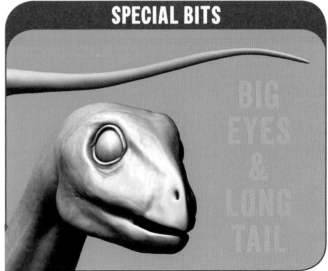

BIG EYES & LONG TAIL

WHAT'S NEXT ?

OTHER EXCITING TITLES AVAILABLE NOW!

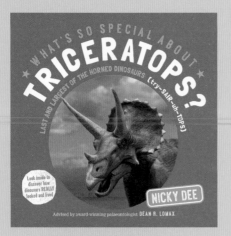

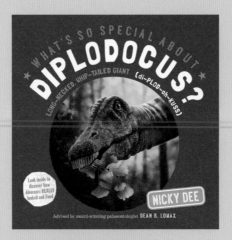

TRICERATOPS
last and largest
of the horned
dinosaurs

DIPLODOCUS
long-necked,
whip-tailed giant

MEGALOSAURUS
the first to
be named

COMING SOON

Velociraptor
turkey-sized, feathered
pack-hunter

Spinosaurus
large, semi-aquatic,
fish-eater

Brachiosaurus
heavy, giraffe-like giant

Maiasaura
motherly, duck-billed
herbivore

Join the 'What's So Special Club'

JOIN OUR FREE CLUB

Download fun dinosaur quizzes and colouring-in sheets
www.specialdinosaurs.com

Enter the exciting world of a 3D artist and discover
how a 3D dinosaur is created and made to look real!

Find out more about our experts and when they
first became fascinated by dinosaurs.

Who is Nicky Dee? Meet the author online.

Join the club and be the first to hear about
exciting new books, activities and games.

Club members will be first in line to order
new books in the series!

COPYRIGHT

ACKNOWLEDGEMENTS

Dean R. Lomax
talented, multiple award-winning
palaeontologist, author and science
communicator and the consultant
for the series   www.deanrlomax.co.uk

David Eldridge and The Curved House
for original book design and artworking

Gary Hanna
thoroughly talented 3D artist

Scott Hartman
skeletons and silhouettes, professional
palaeoartist and palaeontologist

Ian Durneen
skilled digital sketch artist of the
guest dinosaurs

Ron Blakey
Colorado Plateau Geosystems Inc.
creator of the original
paleogeographic maps

My family
patient, encouraging and wonderfully
supportive. Thank you!

To find out more about our artists, designers
and illustrators please visit the website
www.specialdinosaurs.com